simpleSolutions
Kids' Spaces

COLEEN CAHILL

Foreword by Gale C. Steves,
Editor-in-Chief, *Home Magazine*

FRIEDMAN/FAIRFAX
PUBLISHERS

1720 1474
A

Library of Congress Cataloging-in-Publication Data

Cahill, Coleen.
    Kid's spaces / Coleen Cahill ; foreword by Gale C. Steves.
        p. cm. – (Simple solutions)
    Includes bibliographical references and index.
    ISBN 1-56799-929-8 (alk. paper)
    1. Children's rooms. 2. Interior decoration. I. Title. II. Series.

    NK2117.C4 C335 2001
    747.7′7—dc21

                                    00-048431

EDITOR: Sharyn Rosart
ART DIRECTOR: Jeff Batzli
DESIGNER: Lindgren/Fuller Design
PHOTO EDITOR: Kate Perry
PRODUCTION MANAGER: Richela Fabian Morgan

Color separations by Colourscan Overseas Co Pte Ltd
Printed in Hong Kong by C & C Offset Printing Co., Ltd

10 9 8 7 6 5 4 3 2 1

Distributed by Sterling Publishing Company, Inc.
387 Park Avenue South
New York, NY 10016
Distributed in Canada by Sterling Publishing
Canadian Manda Group
One Atlantic Avenue, Suite 105
Toronto, Ontario, Canada M6K 3E7
Distributed in Australia by
Capricorn Link (Australia) Pty Ltd.
P.O. Box 6651
Baulkham Hills, Business Centre, NSW 2153, Australia

Acknowledgements

I'd like to thank several people for their enthusiasm, insight, and helpful advice:
Tim Drew and Gale Steves at *Home Magazine*, Christine Abbate, Timm Brandhorst,
Brian and Chris Cahill, Maureen Cahill, and Leslie Gross. And special thanks to
Kate Perry and Sharyn Rosart at Friedman/Fairfax.

Contents

Foreword

Think back to the house you grew up in. No matter what its true dimensions were, didn't it seem vast, magical, and, at times, mysterious when you were very young? And then, as we grew older, it began to dawn on us that that very same house apparently had been shrinking somehow. Most of our favorite nooks and crannies were losing their charm. And worse, our own rooms one day inexplicably become totally inadequate, especially if they were shared with a sibling whose primary purpose in life, we assumed, was to be the bane of our existence. Who feared monsters under the bed when we were already faced with sharing living space with one? (Fortunately, even such would-be Cains and Abels do mature into the best of friends!)

Despite all those intense childhood feelings, somehow, once we are adults with our own children, we lose sight of how kids perceive their living spaces and what they might expect from them. And, to complicate things just a bit more, we adults will need to remember that those perceptions, expectations, and needs will change, seemingly in the twinkling of an eye. A toddler working his way through the "terrible twos" differs vastly from the same child as an eight-year-old diligently doing his math homework, and even more so from the sixteen-year-old angling to use the car.

Though it might seem hopeless—and hopelessly expensive—to even try to keep up, thankfully there are some basic rules of thumb that will help you stay on an even keel. First, acknowledge and bear in mind that things will change. This will save you from making heavy design investments in elements that will be outgrown in a few short years. Your best course of action is to put your money and creativity into what will grow right along with your children. What this means, for example, is buying furniture that will be as practical for and appealing to your children from the day they start first grade to the day they graduate from high school. A tall order, perhaps, but it is possible. And in the meantime, we can indulge our own and our children's tastes using wallcoverings, colors, and accessories.

One advantage that our children have that perhaps we didn't is that today's homes are, on average, larger than those of a generation ago. This leaves us with a greater opportunity to set up other spaces in the home that will help nurture and broaden their creativity and interests. Space for a computer springs to mind, as well as areas where children can make a mess (without guilt) or complete school projects without having to move everything because someone wants to watch television.

What Simple Solutions: *Kids' Spaces* offers is a compendium of inspiration. Often, in examining what other parents have done to solve their design challenges, we'll find exactly the simple solution that would never have occurred to us. And though we may find ourselves thinking "I wish I'd had that when I was a kid," we do need to remember that we also need to hear our children when they say "I wish I had that," and decide accordingly.

—Gale C. Steves
Editor-in-Chief, *Home Magazine*

Introduction

Children, from newborns to post-college "boomerang" kids, bring a unique and wonderful energy to the home; the flip side is the chaos they can leave in their wake. Designing the different spaces in your home with kids in mind is the best way to reduce the confusion. With a little planning, a home can accommodate the lifestyles of the entire family—right down to its smallest members. The key is to think about the different types of activities that involve children, on their own or in a family setting. It is also important to consider how kids' needs change as they grow. More and more parents are thinking beyond their kids' bedrooms and creating dedicated playrooms, homework areas, snack centers and—for older children—areas that offer privacy and a feeling of independence.

A nursery is typically the first room that parents create for a child, planning color schemes and selecting furniture in loving anticipation of the needs of the room's occupant-to-come. The best nurseries are designed to make both baby and caregiver as comfortable as possible. For baby, the essentials are fairly simple: a crib and changing area, plus ample storage. For the parents, easy access to all necessary items is key. A comfortable place to sit for feedings and playing is equally important. Other major considerations when planning a nursery are light and sound control.

As families grow, it becomes very clear that kids and adults sharing the same home have different needs and interests. Recreation is an obvious example. Similarly, storage is something everyone needs, but kids' storage has to be more accessible and varied. When young children are part of the family, safety is a particularly important issue. Additionally, the various needs of children change as they grow older, which makes planning spaces for kids a real challenge. When designing for children, keep one eye on the present and the other fixed on the future, it'll be here before you know it.

At the other end of the spectrum, kids moving back home after college was first reported as a trend in the early 1990s. This harks back to the days when multiple generations shared one dwelling. The difference this time around is that the returning young adults are often set up in suites that allow them to eat, sleep, and relax in one space. This provides a measure of independence and privacy while still allowing the family to remain connected.

How do you determine the best space for your kids? Start by asking them.

Many kids have definite ideas regarding what they like—even younger children will tell you their favorite color for a bedroom or where they'd like to store their toys. Kids also have opinions about where and how they want to study, relax, or enjoy a snack. As they grow older, they begin to need more and more independence. For decades, young kids have enjoyed playing in home-made forts and tree houses they could call their own, while teens refined their sense of autonomy by declaring their rooms off-limits. Regularly talking to children about how they feel about their spaces is a great way to keep in touch with their changing needs. However, listening to what kids say is only half the equation. It's up to the parents to make choices that will work for the entire family. The best solutions are practical, safe, and affordable decisions that address the needs of the child and make sense for everyone else, too.

Parents have to balance kids' needs with their own vision of how they want their families to live. For example, some parents like to keep activities centrally located so kids can be easily supervised, while others are happy to outfit a play area that's tucked away in a refinished basement. Figure out what will work best for you and your family. Within the parameters that you set, you can give kids a role in designing their own spaces. Getting the whole

family involved will ensure that everyone enjoys the results.

In between bringing a newborn home from the hospital and an adult child returning home to roost, there are shifting needs and changing tastes to be addressed. Most parents react with joy to a child's first steps only to realize seconds later what this new skill means. The little ones can now get around on their own, and a whole new world is within reach. By the time they're in their teens, kids will have a lot to say about how their bedrooms should look and parents have to decide when and if to invest in "real" furniture. Even after the last boomerang kid has moved out, the empty nest may not stay empty for long. Grandchildren are soon ready for sleepovers and the space requirements change once again.

Flexibility and adaptability may be the twin pillars of designing successful spaces for children; careful planning plays a strong supporting role. From bedrooms and bathrooms to playrooms and suites, *Simple Solutions: Kids' Spaces* will inspire you to create functional and fanciful spaces that will grow with your children.

—Coleen Cahill

Bedrooms
Nurseries

Whether you're setting up a nursery in a separate room or making **room for baby** in a cozy corner of your own bedroom, safety is paramount. Infants don't really need a lot of furniture or space, but a **comfortable, secure nursery** will help everyone in the house get a good night's sleep. Sweet dreams!

bright ideas

▶ Window seats

▶ Adjustable shades or blinds for easy light control

▶ Antique armoire for baby's first clothes and beyond

▶ Whimsical knobs and hardware

A comfortable rocking chair is an essential part of any nursery to provide a spot for frequent feedings.

This cozy nursery makes good use of the corner by placing the crib on an angle. The elaborate drapery helps keep out the light and is a decorative focal point of the room. ⌒

Convenience is essential. A changing table near the crib has shelves for storing diapers and tiny outfits. The shelf hanging above has convenient hooks to keep needed items within easy reach. ➲

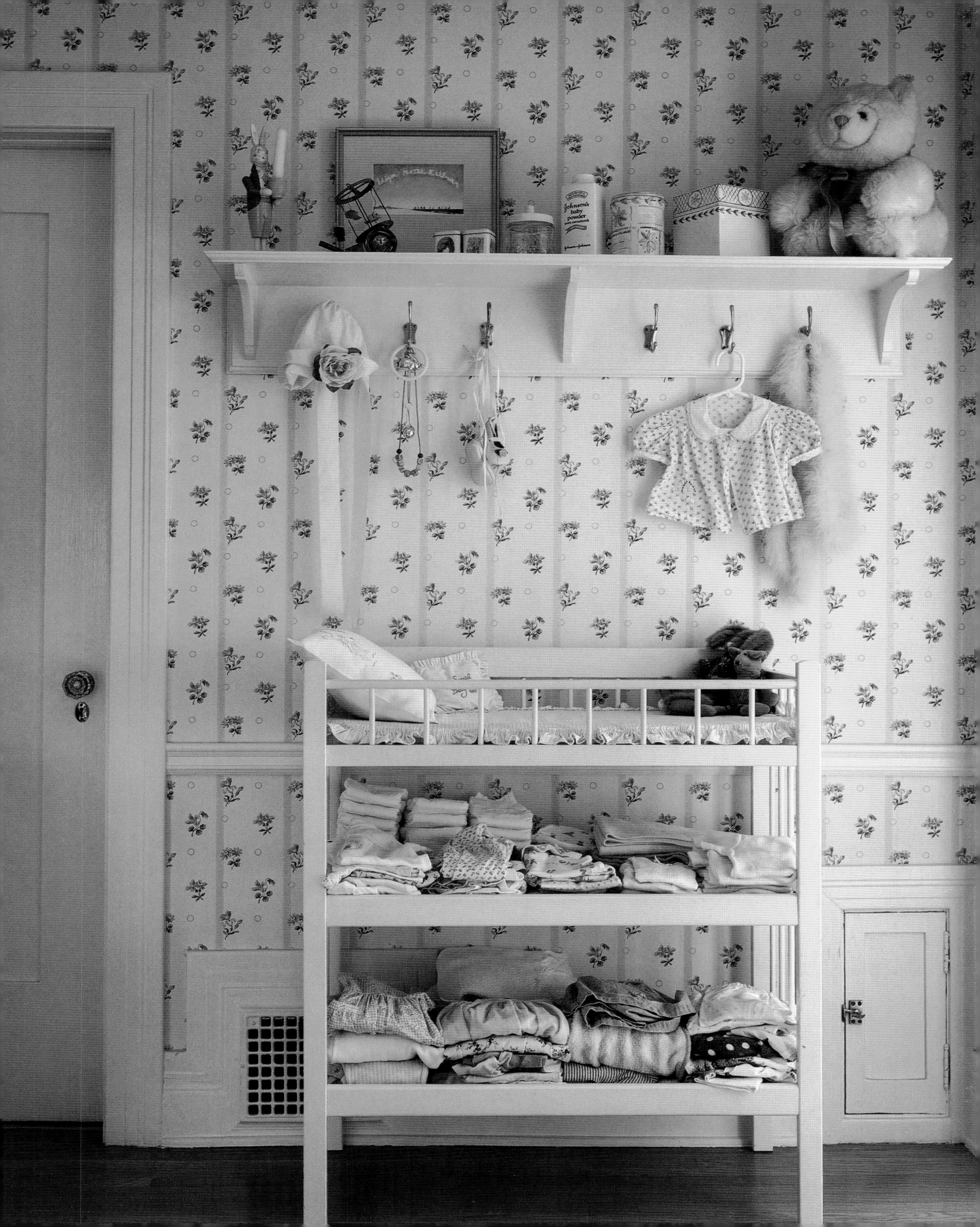
Johnson's
baby
powder
pure cornstarch
Johnson & Johnson

The ample built-in storage in this sunny nursery will come in handy at every stage. Open shelves that can be used for toys or books are combined with cupboards that can store clothing, shoes, and other items. ↻

The cushion lifts up and there is storage beneath the seat.

A built-in window seat offers a cozy spot to sit, perhaps for a parent at feeding time, and eventually for an older child to curl up with a book. ➲

keep in mind

- ☐ If you choose an antique crib, make certain the slats are spaced at the correct distance
- ☐ Choose a crib with a swing-down or swing-out gate to avoid bending over to pick up baby

When the balloon shades are up, a large window lets in plenty of natural light; when it's nap time, however, the substantial weight of the fabric blocks light out.

A crib and a changing table with drawers for storage will suffice for an infant. Grownups require comfortable seating—and a spot for a nap is not a bad idea either. This cozy corner can accommodate all of the above with style.

Creative Beds

When it's time for the little ones to move out of their cribs, parents face a decision about what **type of bed** comes next. Sometimes a guardrail is a good idea until kids are familiar with their new surroundings. Then it's time to have fun. A bed is often the centerpiece of the room, and kids should enjoy crawling into it each night.

bright ideas

▶ Daybeds do double duty for seating and sleeping

▶ Add wheels to beds for ease of movement

▶ Headboards are great for storage

Instead of fabric around the window, horizontal blinds diffuse the light gently.

A bed that suggests a picket fence brings the garden indoors. It's a playful choice that can be enjoyed by children of all ages. A wicker chair and planter continue the garden theme.

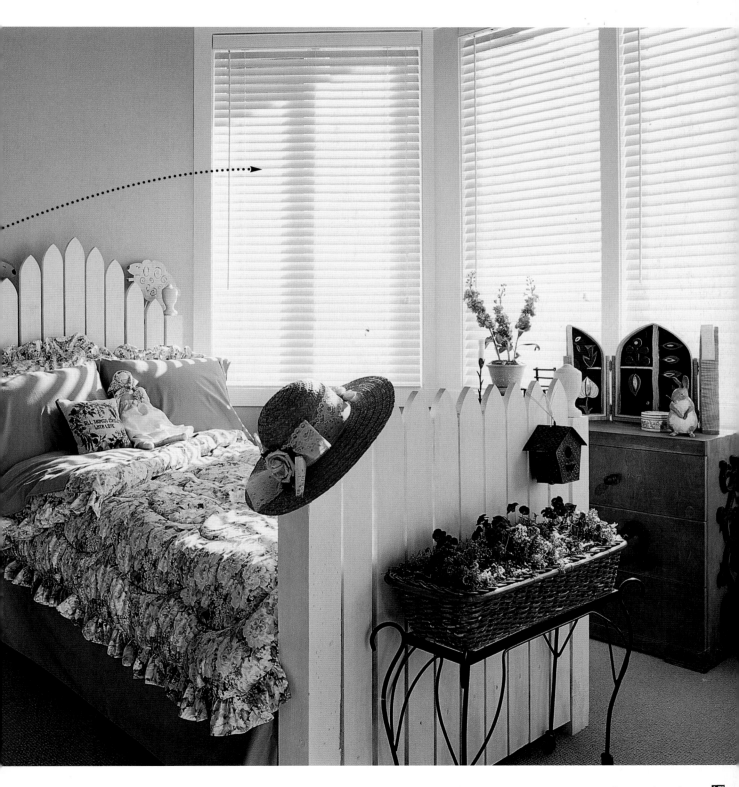

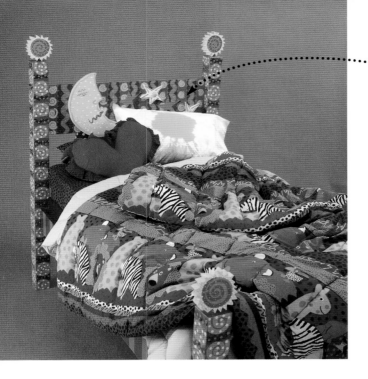

Whimsical paint jobs and fun shapes are easy ways to personalize a kid's bed.

A colorful bed and bedding are bursting with energy. Kids, from toddlers to pre-teens, enjoy playful combinations of colors and imagery. ◖

This bed is eminently practical with a detachable side table and rounded headboard. An open shelf on the lower level of the side table is a super place to store books and other bedtime toys. Brightly colored and patterned bed linens add to the fun. ◓

Nursery rhymes spring to mind as the cat jumps over the moon on this hand-painted bed. Though the shape of the headboard is custom, the bed is a standard twin that can fit into any room. ↻

Hold on to your hat, this custom bed is on the move. The distinctive wave pattern makes a strong statement and is underscored by the combination of midnight blue and natural wood finish. ↑

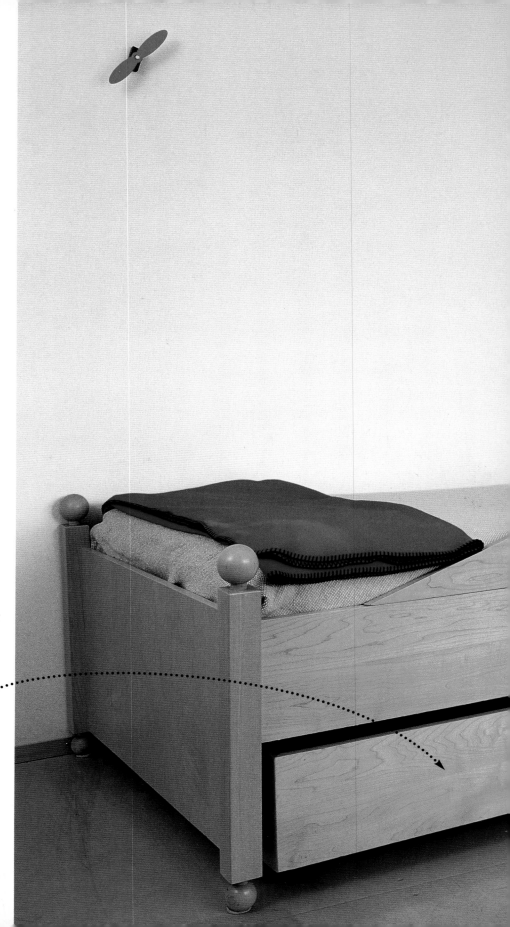

You're never too young for good design. The sculptural shapes of this bed and satellite table are simple enough to appeal to a child yet sufficiently striking to make a design statement. The sliding circle-topped rail serves as a guardrail for younger kids. The attached table suggests a drum and can swing in or away as needed.

A trundle bed pulls out easily from the bottom for sleepovers.

Storage is essential in a child's room—even better when it's incorporated into the bed and night table. The high headboard hides a few secret compartments: bookcases on either side, pullout shelves, and drawers for other essentials. The glass-topped table keeps precious items visible. Drawers have dividers so everything has its own place. ☊

Play out a design theme in easily changed accessories, as in this room's global rug, lamp, and bedlinens.

Form meets function when design also adds flexibility. This sleek rolling bed features large, industrial-style metal and rubber wheels. These come in handy when kids get the urge to rearrange their rooms. ☊

Sharing a Room

T wins, siblings, or just a friend spending the night can mean sharing a bedroom. Before a chalk line appears down the middle of the room, check out the many ways to get two of everything into large and small rooms alike. Plus, there are clever ways to make kids feel like they have their own space even when they are sharing a room.

bright ideas

▶ Create zones: specific areas for dressing, studying, and sleeping

▶ Trundle beds sleep two and save space

▶ Captain's drawers offer discreet storage

Traditional style can work in a child's room, too, as this sunny corner demonstrates. Twin beds, each with its own distinctive quilt, and a play table with several chairs make this charming room easily share-able. ➲

Functional and sleek, these built-in bed units make the most of the space. Each one contains a pull-out desk, three drawers, and open shelving. The built-in storage not only frees up floor space for playing, it also gives each child some space to call his or her own.

FOLLOWING PAGES ➲

Kids need to express themselves: "Welcome to our jungle!" is the message from the twins who occupy these whimsically decorated bunk beds. To play on the natural look of the peeled-log bed, they added a decorative tree and leafy wall stencils. The bedding also features a leaf print. ⊂

Continuing the tree motif are a twig chair and pedestal table. An antique carpenter's toolbox mounted sideways on the wall serves as a display shelf (it could also double as a desk), completing the distinctive personality of this room. ☋

Wall sconces are cleverly placed to provide reading light to each level of the bed.

Bunk beds and a cozy upholstered armchair combine for a clean, tailored look that works at almost any age. Stacking storage boxes in the corner help keep mess to a minimum and add visual interest. ↻

This corner desk makes the most of the compact space, while storage units of similar height are placed on either side of the desk to extend the work surface and hold homework supplies. ☼

A pair of desk lamps provides the right amount of light for homework.

A delightful wall and ceiling mural provides the perfect woodsy backdrop for this log-cabin room. A starry ceiling contributes to the illusion that the sleepers in these cozy bunks are resting under the outdoor skies.

A shelf fashioned after a canoe is a truly special way to store both indoor and outdoor treasures.

Shelves and a bulletin board are clever built-ins at the bottom of the top bunk.

The Wild West has sparked many a young imagination. This décor, chosen by a budding teenager (whose parents approved of the durable furnishings) features a bunk-style daybed, at a right angle to the top bunk, that is perfect for daytime sitting and can also accommodate any overnight "pardners." ❂

Even budding cowboys have to do homework. The freestanding desk and chair provide a serious workspace, while the Western motif is reprised on the lampshade, border, and the metalwork horseshoe hooks on the wall. ♘

Tranquil yet cozy, this large airy room easily holds two white, metal four-poster beds. An expanse of windows and a long window seat offer a perfect spot for daydreaming. ◗

White wicker adds a romantic touch that is nevertheless practical: a wicker trunk at the end of each bed offers additional storage and a chaise provides comfy seating.

A gateleg table between two sleigh beds takes the place of night tables and does double duty as a desk. ↻

Room for Hobbies

T eenagers often take a real interest in the look of their bedrooms, and may even be begging to redecorate in the colors of their favorite sports team. An increased **desire for privacy** may also find teens spending more time in their rooms. There are plenty of good bedroom solutions that match a teen's active lifestyle and **special interests**. Let's hope studying is among them.

bright ideas

▶ Frame favorite posters as inexpensive "art"

▶ Built-in display case for treasures and trophies

▶ Limit thematic decorating to easy-to-change items, such as linens or curtains

Seemingly spare, this room's carefully chosen elements reflect the taste of the young man who inhabits it. An Arts and Crafts-style bed reveals an interest in design. Framed architectural drawings hang on the wall and serve as inspiration, while sports paraphernalia finds its own place. ➲

A drafting table in front of the window can be used for homework and other projects until the budding architect is ready to begin drawing plans.

New furniture can still speak to another era, as does this simple chest in the spirit of the Arts and Crafts movement. A partner to the tall chest, this lower set of drawers provides an accessible surface to display golf and soccer trophies. ↻

Sturdy bins in colorful shades offer portable storage.

Simple furnishings and minimal décor provide the perfect backdrop for a teen who uses the bedroom to display his or her (ever-changing) preoccupations. Here, a fascination with science-fiction is evident. A freestanding shelf offers colorful yet practical storage—and its curvy shape is out of this world. 🎧

The Craftsman-style furniture will surely outlast the sci-fi phase, standing up well to daily wear and tear over the years—and accommodating shifting interests. A trundle bed pulls out should any extraterrestrials spend the night. ☊

A true sports fan is at home in this lovingly assembled shrine of a bedroom, in which everything from the wallpaper to the pillows features the favorite team logo. Simple, sturdy furnishings take a back seat to the current interest, and will easily adapt to the next craze. ⊂

Every teen needs a practical work area. Between two standard chests, a solid surface forms a desktop that's just the right height for writing and other work. A chair is all that's needed to complete the simple solution. ⌒

Ready for Real Furniture

Kids' rooms often mix old and new as they move in and out of phases and their needs change. When and if to invest in real furniture is a purely personal decision, but it can be a good way to create **a unified look** for a room. Another benefit is that when the kids move out, a comfortable guest room is just around the corner.

This room is designed for a pre-teen who plans to stay in it for a while. A wall of windows becomes a light-filled headboard for a full-sized forged metal bed. Ready-to-assemble wooden furniture in a light pickled shade fits neatly under the eaves. ⌒

The bookcase holds toys, and hidden neatly behind closed doors is a computer work center.

A tailored look is just right for the bedroom of a college student who still lives at home. A sleigh bed and ladderback side chair will still work when he sets up his own place. For now, the model aircraft gracing the wall recall the model kits a small boy once loved to assemble. ↻

keep in mind

When buying real furniture:

☐ Think about who will use the room next—
guests, grandchildren—before making
decisions about furniture

☐ If kids plan to take it with them, make choices
that will work in a variety of environments

Fine furniture in a classic style, simple accessories,
and a splash of bold color create a bedroom that is
comfortable for teens, parents, and guests alike,
which adds up to a simple, sensible solution. The
spicy color chosen for the walls offers a vibrant
contrast to the sturdy pine furnishings. ↻

Taking advantage of a wide wall of windows, a built-
in window seat with comfy cushions beckons those
with reading or relaxing on their minds. ➲

A vintage wicker bed frame reminiscent of a rustic lodge from another era sets the tone of this teenager's room. The patterned rug and collection of decorative pillows reflect an interest in Native American culture. ☜

Wall pegs are a must for teens (who might otherwise find the floor a handier place to keep things). The rustic themes of this room continue with the branch pegs and matching rocker, which are both decorative and functional. ☝

Suites

If you have the room, a bedroom suite is an ideal way to give an older child the **independence and privacy** he or she is sure to crave, yet family activities are just steps away. If you're converting an attic or basement room—or even the space above the garage—there are things to consider before you start renovating. Giving kids a role in the design process will ensure that their rooms meet all their needs, from eating and sleeping to studying and working.

bright ideas

- Carpeting to minimize noise
- Wallpaper to cover up less-than-perfect walls
- Light colors will expand a cramped space
- Extra sound-proofing

The window recess forms a canopy for the four-poster bed, while the corner area is made cozy by the addition of an upholstered chair. Carpeting is used throughout the bedroom suite —a simple solution for covering a creaky attic floor.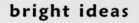

This third-floor attic has been converted into a serene retreat for sleep, study, and solitude: just what a college student needs. Low-ceilinged, the formerly dark and narrow space was transformed by the choice of a Victorian theme that emphasizes romantic florals and a pleasing pastel color palette. ➲

plan ahead

☐ Extend plumbing and heating to spaces that might be converted some day

☐ Plan wiring needs: cable, computer, telephone

☐ Consider internal and external entrances

Almost grown but not yet ready to move all the way out? A spacious studio above a three-car garage becomes semiprivate quarters for a twenty-something eldest child. Masculine yet warm, the décor emphasizes outdoorsy themes. A towering headboard cleverly divides the room into two separate but equally comfortable areas. ↻

Two easy chairs provide seating for guests on the public side of the room. ➲

The space behind the headboard is outfitted with a substantial desk that features a large work surface. The entrance stairs on this side of the room lead down to the kitchen, laundry room, and garage of the main house—so parents can keep an eye on comings and goings. ➲

White ceiling and walls maximize the light—day or night.

Just for Grandkids

Sleeping "dormitories" are an ideal solution when lots of kids are present, whether you enjoy a flock of grandchildren or perhaps a popular family vacation home. If you have a room large enough for **multiple beds,** designating one bedroom especially for kids makes a lot of sense. They'll feel comfortable in a familiar room in their home away from home, and special features like easy-to-reach storage will allow the kids to **settle in** on their own.

bright ideas

▶ Space-saving bunk beds

▶ Portable storage for toys and games

▶ Entertainment center

▶ Homework station

The antique touches in this camp recall the many summers the family has spent on the lake. A room of these long and narrow dimensions provides plenty of space for beds and cribs—and even writing desks—but it's perhaps best at carrying on tradition.

Airy and spare, this space offers plenty of sleeping spots, with four bunks and a large loft above. A walk-in closet and convenient drawers below the bunks provide storage. ↻

*Built-in drawers
below each bed
complement the
shelves above.*

Kids' rooms are perfect for experimenting with imaginative solutions. These knotty pine bunk-style built-in beds offer everything a kid could want, including a bed that doubles as a fort. A recessed bookshelf above each unit holds summer favorites, and a reading light within each curtained cubby allows for undisturbed page-turning. ☊

Bathrooms
Bath Time

Making sure a bathroom works for the smallest members of the family takes some planning. The two most important considerations: **safety and convenience.** Fortunately, there are simple ways of making a bathroom easy for kids to use so bath time can be **good, clean fun!**

A child-height tissue holder is a great idea.

A kids-only bathroom is great for adults and little ones alike. This bathroom was clearly designed with kids in mind. Easy to maintain, it emphasizes function and practicality with lots of built-in storage and plenty of bright lighting. In addition, all the counter edges are rounded for safety. ➲

Towel hooks are ideal for kids, and will help keep towels off the floor.

A particularly kid-friendly feature is a pullout step that lets little ones reach the sink. ☊

An L-shape is eminently practical. In this bathroom, the toilet and a roomy vanity with two sinks form the long arm of the L, while the short arm forms this alcove that holds the tub/shower and keeps them somewhat separate from the rest of the room. This allows more than one child to comfortably use the bathroom at the same time. ➲

Kids call this classic Jack-and-Jill bathroom "neato." Indeed it is. Accessible from two rooms, the cheery bath is extremely functional. Two sinks and lots of counter space eliminate tie-ups on busy mornings. ☛

Plenty of drawers help to eliminate clutter on the countertop, while recessed, mirrored medicine cabinets above offer more storage.

A bi-level vanity makes it safe and easy for smaller kids to reach the sink. Artful handprints provide a splash of color in an otherwise classic white sink. ☊

plan ahead

- ☐ Install showerheads/ faucets with anti- scald controls

- ☐ Think about placement of light switches (consider illuminated switches)

- ☐ Choose slip-resistant surfaces for the floor and shower

As youngsters become teenagers, bath time changes. This bathroom, designed for a pair of teenage sisters, features a vanity with a sink and an area for the sometimes time-consuming process of getting ready. Drawers provide easy storage below and organizers on top of the ceramic tile countertop keep cosmetics and accessories orderly and within reach.

Shared Bathrooms

What happens when all the kids have to **get ready for school** at the same time? That's where bathrooms specifically designed with more than one kid in mind come into play. Separating the sink area from the toilet and bath is a smart solution. Also important: sturdy materials and **lots of storage!**

Cabinets set atop the counter feature tambour doors to keep toiletries convenient yet out of sight.

Pre-teens share this narrow but well-designed bathroom, which is both attractive and extremely functional. A door separates the sink area from the toilet and bathtub/shower so both can be used at the same time. Colorful vinyl flooring, laid in strips of varying width, and deep blue laminate on the countertop are both tough enough to stand up to kids. ➲

In this practical and stylish bath, raising the level of the sinks three inches (7.5cm) above the vanity counter reinforces the his-and-her territories in a bathroom used by two teenagers. ➲

Cubbies hold towels and separate the two cabinet areas. Yellow towels for one teen and white for the other prevent mix-ups.

A giant armoire designed for the guest side offers plenty of storage. It is fixed to the wall although it appears to be a freestanding unit.

With two vanity areas, one on either side of the toilet, this bath meets the tall challenge of satisfying the needs of a six-year-old boy while serving as the guest bath for visitors. An Old West motif, expressed in an age-appropriate style in each vanity area, proves appealing to both child and adult, making for a timeless decorating solution.

This double bath was designed to serve two rooms—a college-aged daughter's bedroom and a guest room. Adjoining the daughter's room is a vanity area, which is in turn attached to a separate room with a toilet and tub/shower. From there, a (lockable) door opens onto a vanity area that adjoins the guest room. ☊

A scallop-edged backsplash echoes the integral white bowl edged in azure Corian with white accents. An integral sink is a cinch to clean. ☝

The overall designs of the two vanities are the same. A large oval mirror above the sink helps visually break up the boxy dimensions of the room, except that the daughter's area has cupboards, while the guest vanity has drawers. ☝

The guest vanity is the mirror image of its counterpart. The lilac and azure hues of the countertop are reversed, and the results are still delightful. ☚

Work and Play
Playing House

A play area that incorporates scaled-down furniture offers kids a **place of their own** where they can spend hours in satisfying play. Kids love the sense of mastery and opportunities for make-believe that are possible when furniture is just the right size. The dimensions of **kid-sized pieces** mean that even in a small room, there is probably a spot for a chair or table that is sized just right for your youngster.

bright ideas

- Furniture on wheels
- Rounded edges on wooden pieces
- Durable, printed fabrics and slipcovers for upholstered pieces
- Storage that kids can reach

An overstuffed loveseat and a pair of chairs are very inviting—especially if you're having an impromptu tea party. The blues used throughout the room create a soothing backdrop, and a trio of large windows floods the play area with natural light. ♫

A dream room for a little girl with lots of imagination, this arrangement offers several distinct areas for playing, with a doll house, a small table and chairs, and a mini-table for bears. A child-sized vanity fits perfectly in front of the bay windows. ☽

This room looks like it was shrunk to size, with each piece scaled down to fit a child. A well-defined play space gives kids the freedom to create their own environment.

A carpeted floor eases the tumbles of the younger set.

Tables, desks, and chairs should be an appropriate height for youngsters, allowing them to work and play comfortably. Lightweight furniture is also a good idea so that it can be easily moved out of the way. ↺

A house within a house. Young children will enjoy exploring the ins and outs of this quaint cottage. Shelves on the first and second floors store books along with favorite toys so that all are within reach. Even on a less grand scale, kids love to have a special place they can make their very own. ➲

Room to Play & Create

Playing is important work for young children, and having the right space helps. An open area and **accessible storage** are essential, and don't forget that the floor is a major play surface for young ones. Planning ahead to ensure that a play area has enough **work surfaces** and adequate lighting will make it easier for kids to get their jobs done.

A pocket door on casters locks in place to protect little ones from venturing down the stairs.

An unfinished attic has been transformed into a playroom that stimulates a child's imagination and fulfills parents' practical needs. To add visual interest, a canopy of lattice strips was applied to the sloped ceiling. The light maple woodwork includes specialized storage solutions throughout the room. ➲

A delightful story-telling niche features child-sized benches framed with dramatic curves and playful cutouts. The arch above the window is straight from a fairy tale. ➲

Attics can make excellent playrooms. They are out of the way of the home's main traffic routes, and their typically low, sloped ceilings pose no problems for kids. Here, an oval window lets in much-needed light. Recessed bulbs supplement the natural light and provide task lighting for the children and their furry friends.

Wood floors are resilient and easy to keep clean.

A simple décor, as in this white-painted, wooden-floored playroom, allows toys and kids' artwork to form the decoration. Lots of open floor space is essential, as the floor provides the primary staging area for many children's games. ↻

A built-in desk provides a spot for a computer and an additional work surface for arts and crafts.

Materials are mixed and matched on this clever chalk-bulletin-paper board. Each of the three houses offers a different surface for kids to express themselves and display their creative work. ☊

Packed to the rafters
with good ideas, this
playroom has comfy
window seats to
encourage reading,
child-sized furniture, a
magnetic bulletin board,
and in the center of it
all, recessed storage to
hold toys, books,
and more.

Dividing Space

Not every home contains a room just for the kids. A clearly defined play area can be carved from almost any space, however. And if you are lucky enough to have a playroom, dividing it into **activity areas** will help kids feel more comfortable and competent in their own environments. It helps when related activities are placed nearby each other. Plus, a **well-organized space** will make clean-up easier.

bright ideas

- ▶ Movable screens and panels
- ▶ Functional surfaces like chalk or cork
- ▶ Bookshelves as dividers

Attractive wood panels serve as a divider to create a kids' play and dining area that is separate from the main room. Parents can still keep an eye on things, however, and the panels can be moved easily in order to use the entire room.

This playroom was designed with the future in mind. Modeled after a library, it will easily adapt to the activities of older children. For now, the central play area provides a table for art projects, games, snacks and reading. ↻

The shelving unit is open, making books and toys accessible from either side.

Matched bookcases on either side of the play area zone off two mini-workstations, so more than one child can work quietly while others play on the other side of the bookcase. A classic library ladder mounted on a curving rail rolls from one bookcase to another, making it easy to reach books and toys stored on high shelves. ↺

On the other side of the doors, active play is in full swing. Shelving that holds games, toys, and the TV is an integral part of the décor. ↻

Even the doors do double duty, surfaced in whiteboard and chalkboard on one side.

A large work/play space has been divided into two zones using clever pocket doors. On the serious side, a built-in desk with storage was designed for computers and other quiet tasks that require a smooth work surface. ↻

Time to Study

C rayons and paint will eventually give way to books and computers, as kids begin to bring **homework** from school. Every child needs an efficient space to work. Whether you plan to incorporate a homework area into a bedroom or create a distinct **study space,** there's a checklist of good ideas from wiring to lighting that will help ensure the space works the way you need it to. Checking on the homework is another matter.

bright ideas

▶ Ergonomic furniture that grows with child

▶ Roll-out keyboard trays

▶ Indirect lighting minimizes screen glare

▶ File drawers on wheels

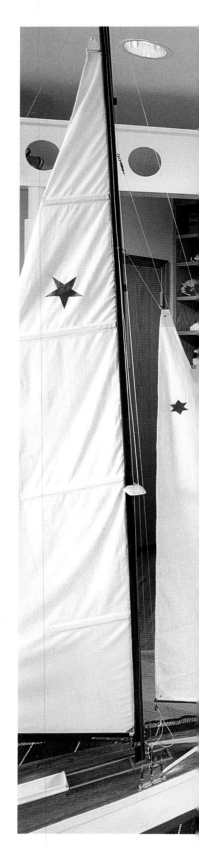

A floor-to-ceiling wall unit designed for a teen provides a convenient work surface and ample storage opportunities. The desk is compact with open cubbies above for easy access. The taller cupboards on either side are ideal for clothing and sports equipment.

Today, even a fishing camp is not complete without a computer. A junior fisherman has the ideal desk that combines everything he needs to get his schoolwork done with plenty of display space for his collections. ↻

Bulletin boards allow kids to pin up mementos, notes, and other paraphernalia without damaging walls.

A small but efficient study area fits perfectly into a nook tucked at one end of a hallway. The combined desk/shelving unit is traditional in style and complements the home's décor while providing space for books and a useful work surface. The student is sufficiently separated from the home's main activities to be able to concentrate, but parents can still supervise. ↻

A second-story landing was enlarged to accommodate a study place for two kids. The parents like that it's easily accessible for supervision and the kids like the light-filled and open feeling of the workspace. Two computers share a clean desk surface and the keyboards are side-by-side on a roll-out tray. ↻

A window shade eliminates glare, an important consideration for computer users.

When space is limited, every inch needs to be used. Here, a corner was fitted out with a computer workstation. A filing cabinet on casters is tucked under the desk, and a small bookcase/storage cabinet provides both open and hidden storage. The result is a compact, efficient space. ➲

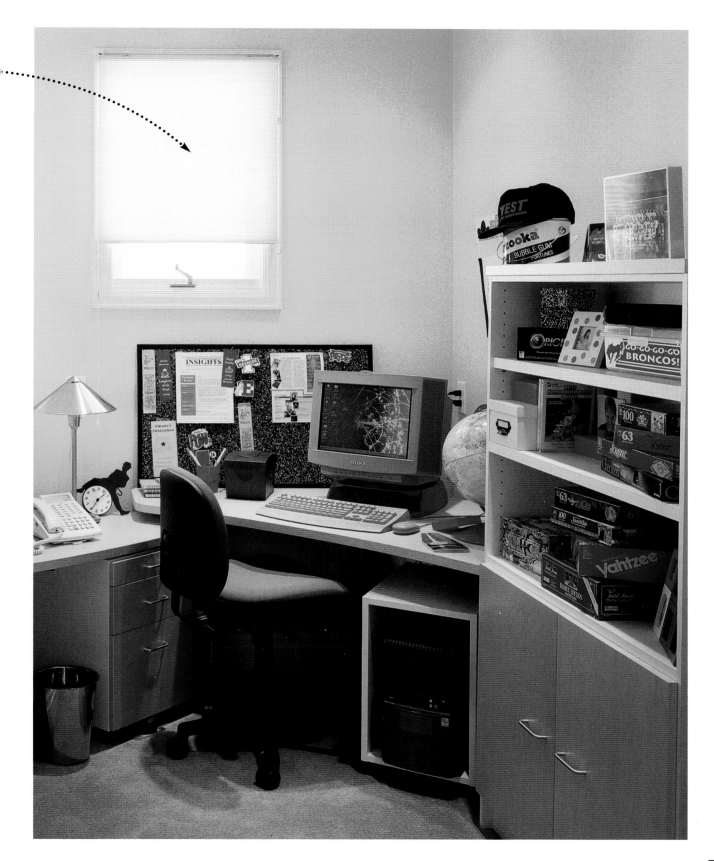

A two-way bookcase is designed to be reachable from both desk and bed.

When space is unlimited, get creative. A large bedroom can include a homework/storage area with lots of features. This collection of playfully arranged storage units includes a desk that adjusts in one-inch increments to elevate from a child-sized 25 inches (62.5cm) to a maximum adult-sized 30 inches (75cm). Above the desk is a handy wraparound bulletin board. ↻

The latest computer desk design combines simple Scandinavian style with comfort and good ergonomics. An added bonus is the way it fits perfectly into a tight corner. 🎧

Hanging Out

Creating a kid-friendly area just for **relaxing** may seem like a luxury, but many families find it's the most effective solution. Older kids need play spaces just as much as their younger siblings. For teens, that probably means a comfy sofa, television, and maybe a computer. With a little planning, a hang-out room can double as an extra bedroom or evolve into a space the **whole family** can enjoy.

bright ideas

▶ Use washable fabrics such as fleece

▶ Easy-to-clean flooring: tile, wood, vinyl

▶ Oversized floor pillows

▶ Sleeper sofas

Under the alcove that holds the wide-screen television is a pull-out project table that opens three ways, and two handy roll-out chests of drawers.

Its owners call this room "the kitchen of the mind," a place for the entire family to come together, interact, and relax. A floor-to-ceiling cabinet system provides ample storage. Behind the rolling bookcase is a Murphy bed that lets the room do double duty as a guest room.

A loft designed just for the younger set overlooks the
family and breakfast rooms and is connected to the
children's bedrooms. Its location gives kids privacy
yet keeps them connected. A television is available,
but so is a big table just the right size for puzzles and
other projects. ⌒

A shared workstation is a great option for a family with two or more kids. The key to making it work is a large work surface, plus as much storage as possible—here, cupboards, cubbies, and adjustable shelves provide many storage options and help contain clutter. ☊

Don't forget the possibilities offered by a garage—the unused bay in this one was transformed into a 14-by-28-foot (4.2 x 8.4m) project room for a college student who comes home on weekends. A wall of blue-stained maple cabinets stores everything from books to sporting equipment. The vinyl floor ensures a comfortable, durable, and easy-to-clean surface. ◗

Open-sided shelves on wheels hold painting supplies that need to be moved around the room.

If you have an unused corner, a freestanding desk outfitted with a computer and any other equipment can serve as an efficient workstation to be shared by all the members of the family. 𝛀

Child-friendly decorating can be stylish. This large room accommodates children and adults equally. One wall is devoted to built-in open storage. It makes toys easier to find and encourages children to tidy up, too. The children's possessions become decorative elements in their own right. ☰

Colorful, pull-out plastic bins are ideal for holding small toys.

The other end of the playroom is more grown up. Adults congregate around the fireplace, which is flanked by glass-doored cabinets that display collections out of children's reach. ☊

A futon sofa opens up for overnight guests.

Tired of kids tracking snacks from kitchen to TV room? A home entertainment unit is turned into a snack center for the kids by fitting a microwave in the adjustable shelving. ⌒

A teen retreat is welcomed by kids and grown-ups alike. This space serves as an extension of the bedrooms for entertaining, studying, or just plain relaxing. It was deliberately closed off from the living area below to contain noise and give both parents and teens some privacy. ➲

Storage Solutions

Shelves in All Shapes & Sizes

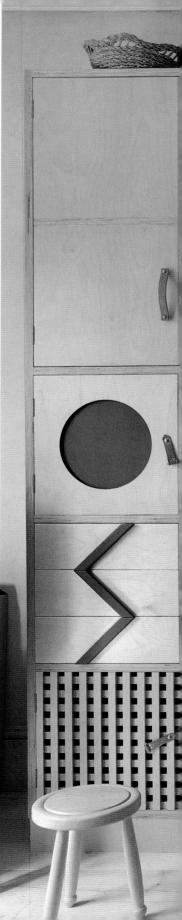

Kids are always accumulating stuff. Finding the room to store it all—and make it look attractive—can be a challenge. **Creative storage** should provide opportunities both to display and to conceal items. The best part is that good, accessible storage will help kids learn the value of organizing their stuff and keeping their spaces **clean and tidy.**

bright ideas

- Under-bed storage
- Window seats that lift up
- Varied shelf heights
- Cubbyholes
- Baskets

This oversized custom drawer-and-cubbyhole wall unit turns storage into a game. The combination of shelves, cubbies, and boxy cupboards helps young children organize while adding visual interest to the room.

An all-in-one bed/storage unit is ideal when space is at a premium. This unit combines shelves for books and collectibles and a pull-out closet with deep cubbies and a rack for hanging clothes. ○

Space is limited in this room because of the sloping ceiling, so creative thinking was called for and resulted in innovative storage solutions. The bunk-style bed is a marvel of efficiency. From beneath it slides out a substantial work surface with built-in shelves, in addition to three drawers alongside. ⊃

In a bedroom created by converting a dormer, built-in bookshelves make clever use of a tight corner while adding an interesting architectural element to the room. For nooks and crannies that can't accommodate freestanding units, built-in shelves are an excellent solution. ↻

Note the antique door and decorative doorframe, simple ways to add character to new construction.

Kids love to display their toys and treasures. In this unit, shelves of different heights accommodate a variety of items and add visual interest. When organizing, place items used frequently and non-breakables on the lower shelves. ➲

This wall of shelves is both functional and fun. An integral part of the room's design, the center section is actually a door to an adjoining room. Shelves of varying heights are ideal for books of all sizes, while plush toys find a convenient home on the shallow center unit. ◖

Shelves that are too shallow to provide extensive storage make excellent display surfaces. A trio of nesting baskets placed individually on the shelves expand the storage options and keep items like casual clothing well organized and easily accessible. ◑

Incorporating a low bookshelf into this living room provides accessible storage for children's toys, books, and games while helping to define a play area. The light seafoam green of the bookshelf complements the cool blue walls and works wonderfully with the painting above.

Let's Get Organized

Young children actually enjoy **sorting and organizing** tasks. Capitalize on this when creating your storage plans. Kids will function more efficiently when everything they need is close at hand. It lets them easily shift from one activity to the next—and finding the right toys becomes **part of the fun.**

bright ideas

▶ Stackable crates
▶ Color-coded bins
▶ Wire shelves and drawers
▶ Peg racks and hooks

Stepped storage "garages" house everything from a beanbag chair to a teepee. These oversized units allow kids to stow their bigger toys behind colorful shades that become an important decorative element. ⌒

The colorful shades hide clutter and add a whimsical touch to the room—and they're easy for small hands to operate. ➲

Plastic storage boxes keep a child's collections and treasures well organized; they can be stacked on bookshelves when not in use. Lettered with permanent pen for easy identification, the boxes can be easily retrieved and their contents enjoyed. (Color coded boxes are another good method of organizing.)

*Pole and shelf
heights can be
easily adjusted.* ⋯⋯⋯⋯

With clever accessories, an active child's desk becomes an extremely efficient storage unit. Drawers, hanging paper racks, banner paper, and stretch cords are simple ways to improve the functionality of a desk while helping to teach organizational skills and responsibility for a work space. ↻

This closet makes maximum use of both vertical and horizontal storage space through a combination of poles and shelves. It's a good idea to organize a closet so that a youngster can reach easily at least one pole's length of clothing. ➲

Resources

Information

If you are interested in hiring a qualified professional to help with a remodeling job or new construction, here is a list of design and planning resources that may be helpful:

American Institute of Architects (AIA)–When making structural changes, an architect should be considered. Many, but not all, architects belong to The American Institute of Architects. Call (202) 626-7300 for information and the phone number of your local chapter. www.aiaonline.com

The American Society of Interior Designers (ASID)–An interior designer can provide helpful advice, especially when you are remodeling an existing space. The American Society of Interior Designers represents more than 20,000 professionally qualified interior designers. Call ASID's client/referral service at (800) 775-ASID. www.asid.org

National Association of the Remodeling Industry (NARI)–When it's time to select a contractor to work on your project, you might consider a member of the National Association of the Remodeling Industry. Call (800) 611-6274 for more information. www.nari.org

National Association of Home Builders (NAHB)–When you're looking at builders to construct a new home, contact the National Association of Home Builders. Call (800) 368-5242 for more information. www.nahb.org

The following manufacturers, associations and resources may be helpful as you plan rooms with children in mind:

Juvenile Products Manufacturers Association offers a free 16-page non-manufacturer specific brochure, titled *Safe & Sound for Baby*, illustrating proper use of many juvenile products. Visit www.jpma.org or send a SASE to:

JPMA Public Information
236 Rt. 38 West
Suite 100
Moorestown, NJ 08057

Another source for product safety information is the US Consumer Product Safety Commission, which can be reached at 800 638 2772 or www.cpsc.gov

Products

BATHROOM FAUCETS/ FIXTURES/SHOWERS/ TUBS/ACCESSORIES

American Standard
(800) 524-9797
www.americanstandard
us.com

Aqua Glass
(901) 632-2501
www.aquaglass.com

Delta
(800) 345-DELTA
www.deltafaucet.com

Grohe
(630) 582-7711
www.grohe.com

Kohler
(800) 4-KOHLER
www.kohlerco.com

Lasco
(800) 877-2005
www.lascobathware.com

Moen
(800) BUY-MOEN
www.moen.com

Swan
(800) 325-7008
www.theswancorp.com

Universal-Rundle
(800) 955-0316
www.universal-
rundle.com

FLOORING

Italian Trade
    Commission
Ceramic Tile Department
499 Park Avenue
New York NY 10022
(212) 980-1500
www.italtrade.com

Trade Commission of
    Spain
Ceramic Tile Department
2655 Le Jeune Road
Suite 114
Coral Gables, FL 33134
(305) 446-4387
www.tilespain.com

National Wood Flooring
    Association
16388 Westwoods
    Business Park
Ellisville, MO 63021
(800) 422-4556
www.woodfloors.org

www.floorfacts.com
(a global directory that
helps consumers explore
flooring options)

FURNISHINGS, STORAGE SOLUTIONS, WALL COVERINGS, AND ACCESSORIES

Bellini
www.bellini.com

Anna French, Ltd.
available in US through
Classic Revivals, Inc.
(617) 574-9030
www.classicrevivals.com

California Closets
(800) 336-9189
www.calclosets.com

Crate & Barrel
(800) 967-6696
www.crateandbarrel.com

Eisenhart Wall Coverings
(800) 726-3267
www.eisenhartwall
coverings.com

Ethan Allen
www.ethanallen.com

Hold Everything
(800) 840-3596
www.holdeverything.com

Ikea
(800) 225-IKEA
www.ikea.com

Imperial Wall Coverings
(800) 539-5399
www.imp-wall.com

JC Penney
(800) 222-6161
www.jcpenney.com

Lands' End
(800) 963-4816
www.landsend.com

Lexington Home
Furnishings
(800) 539-4636
www.lexington.com

LL Bean
(800) 441-5713
www.llbean.com

Mitchell Gold Company
(800) 789-5401
www.mitchellgold.com

Pottery Barn Kids
(800) 430-7373
www.potterybarnkids.
com

Sauder Furniture
(800) 523-3987
www.sauder.com

Scott Jordan Furniture
(212) 620-4682
www.scottjordan.com

Sears
(800) 549-4505
www.sears.com

Spiegel
(800) SPIEGEL
www.spiegel.com

Thomasville
(800) 927-9202
www.thomasville.com

Waverly
(800) 423-5881
www.waverly.com

LIGHTING

American Lighting
    Association
P.O. Box 420288
Dallas, TX 75342-0288
(800) 274 4484
www.americanlighting
assoc.com

PAINT

Benjamin Moore
(800) 6 PAINT 6
www.benjaminmoore.
com

Dutch Boy
(800) 828-5669
www.dutchboy.com

Pratt & Lambert
www.prattandlambert.
com

Sherwin-Williams
(800) 474-3794
www.sherwin-
williams.com

WINDOWS, DOORS AND COVERINGS

Andersen
(800) 426-4261
www.andersenwindows.
com

Hunter Douglas Window
Fashions
(800) 937-7895
www.hunterdouglas.com

Loewen
(800) 245-2295
www.loewen.com

Marvin
(800) 241-9450
www.marvin.com

Morgan
(800) 877-9482
www.morgandoors.com

Pella
(800) 54-PELLA
www.pella.com

Pozzi
(800) 257-9663
www.pozzi.com

Photo Credits

©**Courtesy of Anna French Limited**, Boston, MA: 118, 119; ©**Laurie Black:** 16–17 (Catherine Gerry Interiors), 92–93 (Catherine Gerry Interiors), 106–107 (Catherine Gerry Interiors); ©**Judith Bromle**y: 76 (Kathryn Quinn, Architect), 77 (Kathryn Quinn, Architect); ©**Steven Brooke:** 40 (Barbara Dalton, Designer, ASID), 41 (Barbara Dalton, Designer, ASID), 44 (Charles Riley, Designer), 45 (Charles Riley, Designer), 48 (Slifer Designs), 49 (Slifer Designs), 52 (Slifer Designs), 53 top (Slifer Designs), 53 bottom (Slifer Designs), 60, 61, 65 (Slifer Designs), 68, 69 top left, 69 top right, 69 bottom, 95, 100 (Slifer Designs), 101 (Slifer Designs), 102–103 (Charles Riley, Designer), 103 (Charles Riley, Designer), 104 (Joanna Lombard & Denis Hector, Architects), 105 (Joanna Lombard & Denis Hector, Architects), 106 (Barbara Dalton, Designer, ASID); ©**Carlos Domenech:** 32–33 (Taylor & Taylor, Designers); ©**Elizabeth Whiting & Associates:** 26–27, 110, 110–111; ©**Lois Ellen Frank:** 122, 123; ©**David** Frazier: 66–67 (Candice Schiller, Designer); ©**Michael Garland:** 20–21 (Alla Kazovsky, Designer), 22–23 (Alla Kazovsky, Designer), 23 (Alla Kazovsky, Designer), 72–73 (Designed by Pasadena Showcase), 74 (Carey Berg, Designer), 96, 98–99 (Alla Kazovsky, Designer); ©**Tria Giovan:** 9, 115; ©**Kari Haavisto:** 28 (Designed by Suzanne Felber of Memory Merchandising), 29 (Designed by Suzanne Felber of Memory Merchandising), 38 (Designed by Diane Mallory of Design Studio at Gabberts), 39 (Designed by Diane Mallory of Design Studio at Gabberts), 93 (Designed by Diane Mallory of Design Studio at Gabberts), 94 (Designed by Suzanne Felber of Memory Merchandising); **Interior Archive:** ©Fritz von der Schulenburg: 84–85, 108–109; ©**Michael Jensen:** 46 (Lisa Reindorf, AIA, Goldman Reindorf Architects), 47 (Lisa Reindorf, AIA, Goldman Reindorf Architects); ©**image/dennis krukowski:** 14–15 (Designed by Pearl Thompson of Nursery Lines, NYC); ©**James Levin:** 18 top, 18 bottom, 19 top, 19 bottom; ©**Jeff McNamara:** 34, 35, 42–43 (Patricia Stadel, Designer, ASID), 43 (Patricia Stadel, Designer, ASID), 50 (Designed by Claudia Judelman of Laura Ashley), 51 (Designed by Claudia Judelman of Laura Ashley), 64; ©**Robert Perron:** 56 (Robert Knight, Architect, Blue Hill, ME); ©**Phillip H. Ennis Photography:** 82–83 (Reger Designs); ©**George Ross:** 58, 59 left, 59 right (all designed by Aura Bershad Pressman & Nadine Nemec of A.B.I.D.); ©**Eric Roth:** 2, 70, 116–117, 120–121; ©**Samu Studios:** 12, 13, 36 (Courtesy of Hearst Specials), 75, 88 (Lee Najman Design), 89 (Lee Najman Design); ©**Brad Simmons:** 62–63 (Delia Spradley, Designer, Friendswood, TX), 78–79 (Phyllis Craver, Designer, Powell, OH); ©**William P. Steele:** 30 (Architectural Design by Lindal Cedar Homes), 31 (Architectural Design by Lindal Cedar Homes), 97 (Architectural Design by Lindal Cedar Homes); ©**Tim Street-Porter:** 10 (Tom Callaway, Designer), 11 (Tom Callaway, Designer), 81, 86 (Heidi Hefferlin, Architect), 87 (Heidi Hefferlin, Architect), 113; ©**Brian Vanden Brink:** 54–55; ©**Peter Vitale:** 37 (Michael Foster Designs); ©**Dominique Vorillon:** 24–25 (Robin Piconne, Designer/Homeowner); ©**Jessie Walker Associates:** 6, 57, 71, 90–91; ©**William Wyman for CDMA, Inc.:** 112 (Chris Cahill, Designer)

Index

MAR 2002